رمضان كريم

RAMADAN

Planner

THIS BOOK BELONGS TO :

_____

_____

_____

شَهْرُ رَمَضَانَ ٱلَّذِىٓ أُنزِلَ فِيهِ ٱلْقُرْءَانُ هُدًى لِّلنَّاسِ وَبَيِّنَـٰتٍ مِّنَ ٱلْهُدَىٰ وَٱلْفُرْقَانِ ۚ فَمَن شَهِدَ مِنكُمُ ٱلشَّهْرَ فَلْيَصُمْهُ ۖ وَمَن كَانَ مَرِيضًا أَوْ عَلَىٰ سَفَرٍ فَعِدَّةٌ مِّنْ أَيَّامٍ أُخَرَ ۗ يُرِيدُ ٱللَّهُ بِكُمُ ٱلْيُسْرَ وَلَا يُرِيدُ بِكُمُ ٱلْعُسْرَ وَلِتُكْمِلُوا۟ ٱلْعِدَّةَ وَلِتُكَبِّرُوا۟ ٱللَّهَ عَلَىٰ مَا هَدَىٰكُمْ وَلَعَلَّكُمْ تَشْكُرُونَ

{The month of Ramadhan [is that] in which was revealed the Qur'an, a guidance for the people and clear proofs of guidance and criterion. So whoever sights [the new moon of] the month, let him fast it; and whoever is ill or on a journey – then an equal number of other days. Allah intends for you ease and does not intend for you hardship and [wants] for you to complete the period and to glorify Allah for that [to] which He has guided you; and perhaps you will be grateful.}

[Quran 2:185]

Contents

1- Ramadan Days Tracker

2- Ramadan Goals

3- Quran Tracker

4- Ramadan Planner With Daily Hadith and Gratitude Dua

5- A Dua a Day and Notes

6- Iftar Party Planner

7- Aid Préparation

Ramadan Days Tracker

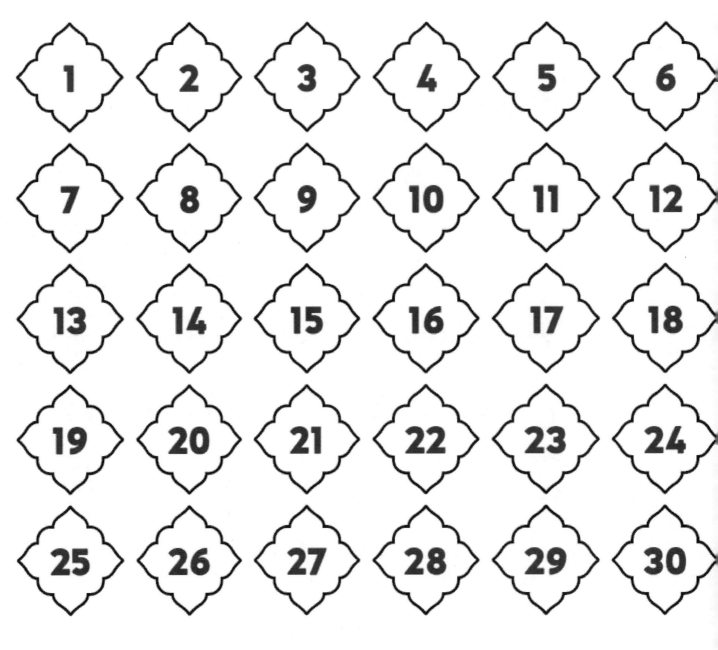

Ramadan Goals

Salah

Quran

Zakat

Other Good Deeds

Quran Tracker

Day	Surah	From ayat	To ayat

Quran Tracker

Day	Surah	From ayat	To ayat

Ramadan Day 1

Daily Schedule

Morning

....
....
....

Afternoon

....
....
....

Evening

....
....
....

Night

....
....
....

Sunnah Habits

○ Morning Dhikr   ○ Exercise   ○ Eat Healthy   ○ Give to Charity
○ Evening Dhikr   ○ 8 Glass of Water   ○ Balanced Varied Iftar

○ Fajr
○ Asr
○ Isha'a
○ Dhuhr
○ Maghrib
○ Taraweeh

Alhamdulillah for witnessing Ramadan.
Allah's Messenger ﷺ said,
"When Ramadan begins, the gates of Paradise are opened."
(Hadith; Bukhari 1898)

Todays Goals

○ ....
○ ....
○ ....
○ ....
○ ....

Iftar & Suhour Meal Planner

Iftar

....

....

....

....

Suhoor

....

....

....

....

To Do List

....

....

....

....

....

....

....

....

How Can I Make Tomorrow Better?

....

....

Daily Reflections

....

....

....

....

....

....

Rate Your Day ☆ ☆ ☆ ☆ ☆

Ramadan Day 2

Daily Schedule

Morning
....
....
....

Afternoon
....
....
....

Evening
....
....
....

Night
....
....
....

○ Fajr

○ Asr

○ Isha'a

○ Dhuhr

○ Maghrib

○ Taraweeh

Alhamdulillah for being on the right path. The Messenger of Allah ﷺ said, "He who calls others to follow the Right Guidance will have a reward equal to the reward of those who follow him, without their reward being diminished in any respect on that account."
(Hadith; Riyad as-Salihin 1382)

Todays Goals

○ ....

○ ....

○ ....

○ ....

○ ....

Sunnah Habits

○ Morning Dhikr   ○ Exercise   ○ Eat Healthy   ○ Give to Charity

○ Evening Dhikr   ○ 8 Glass of Water   ○ Balanced Varied Iftar

Iftar & Suhour Meal Planner

Iftar

....
....
....
....

Suhoor

....
....
....
....

To Do List

....
....
....
....

....
....
....
....

How Can I Make Tomorrow Better?

....
....

Daily Reflections

....
....
....
....
....

Rate Your Day ☆ ☆ ☆ ☆ ☆

Ramadan Day 3

Daily Schedule

Morning
....
....
....

Afternoon
....
....
....

Evening
....
....
....

Night
....
....
....

○ Fajr

○ Asr

○ Isha'a

○ Dhuhr

○ Maghrib

○ Taraweeh

Alhamdulillah for shelter.
Anas reported Allah's Messenger ﷺ as
saying: When you go to bed, say: "Praise is
to Allah Who fed us, provided us drink,
sufficed us and provided us with shelter, f
many a people there is none to suffice an
none to provide shelter."
(Hadith; Muslim 2715)

Todays Goals

○ ....
○ ....
○ ....
○ ....
○ ....

Sunnah Habits

○ Morning Dhikr   ○ Exercise   ○ Eat Healthy   ○ Give to Charity
○ Evening Dhikr   ○ 8 Glass of Water ○ Balanced Varied Iftar

Iftar & Suhour Meal Planner

Iftar

....

....

....

....

Suhoor

....

....

....

....

To Do List

....

....

....

....

....

....

....

....

How Can I Make Tomorrow Better?

....

....

Daily Reflections

....

....

....

....

....

....

Rate Your Day ☆ ☆ ☆ ☆ ☆

Ramadan Day 4

Daily Schedule

Morning
....
....
....

Afternoon
....
....
....

Evening
....
....
....

Night
....
....
....

- ○ Fajr
- ○ Asr
- ○ Isha'a
- ○ Dhuhr
- ○ Maghrib
- ○ Taraweeh

Alhamdulillah for food and drink
Prophet ﷺ said: "A grateful
eater is equal to a patient
fasting person."
(Hadith; Ibn Majah 127)

Todays Goals

- ○ ....
- ○ ....
- ○ ....
- ○ ....
- ○ ....

Sunnah Habits

- ○ Morning Dhikr
- ○ Evening Dhikr
- ○ Exercise
- ○ 8 Glass of Water
- ○ Eat Healthy
- ○ Balanced Varied Iftar
- ○ Give to Charity

Iftar & Suhour Meal Planner

Iftar

....
....
....
....

Suhoor

....
....
....
....

To Do List

....
....
....
....

....
....
....
....

How Can I Make Tomorrow Better?

....
....

Daily Reflections

....
....
....
....
....

Rate Your Day ☆ ☆ ☆ ☆ ☆

Ramadan Day 5

Daily Schedule

Morning

....
....
....

Afternoon

....
....
....

Evening

....
....
....

Night

....
....
....

○ Fajr
○ Asr
○ Isha'a
○ Dhuhr
○ Maghrib
○ Taraweeh

Alhamdulillah for my family and friend
Abu Mas'ud reported Allah's Messeng
ﷺ as saying: "When a Muslim spend
on his family seeking reward for it fr
Allah, it counts for him as sadaqah."
(Hadith; Muslim 1002a)

Todays Goals

○ ....
○ ....
○ ....
○ ....
○ ....

Sunnah Habits

○ Morning Dhikr   ○ Exercise   ○ Eat Healthy   ○ Give to Charity
○ Evening Dhikr   ○ 8 Glass of Water ○ Balanced Varied Iftar

Iftar & Suhour Meal Planner

Iftar

....

....

....

....

Suhoor

....

....

....

....

To Do List

....

....

....

....

....

....

....

....

How Can I Make Tomorrow Better?

....

....

Daily Reflections

....

....

....

....

....

....

Rate Your Day ☆ ☆ ☆ ☆ ☆

Ramadan Day 6

Daily Schedule

Morning

....
....
....

Afternoon

....
....
....

Evening

....
....
....

Night

....
....
....

Sunnah Habits

○ Fajr
○ Asr
○ Isha'a
○ Dhuhr
○ Maghrib
○ Taraweeh

Alhamdulillah for education. The Prophet ﷺ said, "The best among you (Muslims) are those who learn the Qur'an and teach it." (Hadith; Bukhari 5027)

Todays Goals

○ ....
○ ....
○ ....
○ ....
○ ....

○ Morning Dhikr   ○ Exercise   ○ Eat Healthy   ○ Give to Charity
○ Evening Dhikr   ○ 8 Glass of Water   ○ Balanced Varied Iftar

Iftar & Suhour Meal Planner

Iftar

....

....

....

....

Suhoor

....

....

....

....

To Do List

....

....

....

....

....

....

....

....

How Can I Make Tomorrow Better?

....

....

Daily Reflections

....

....

....

....

....

Rate Your Day ☆ ☆ ☆ ☆ ☆

Ramadan Day 7

Daily Schedule

Morning

....

....

....

Afternoon

....

....

....

Evening

....

....

....

Night

....

....

....

○ Fajr

○ Asr

○ Isha'a

○ Dhuhr

○ Maghrib

○ Taraweeh

Alhamdulillah for the way Almighty made
Abu Huraira reported Allah's Messenger ﷺ
as saying: "Allah is self-respecting and
believer is also self-respecting and the
respect of Allah is injured if a believer d
what He has forbidden him to do."
(Hadith; Muslim 2761a)

Todays Goals

○ ....

○ ....

○ ....

○ ....

○ ....

Sunnah Habits

○ Morning Dhikr   ○ Exercise   ○ Eat Healthy   ○ Give to Charity

○ Evening Dhikr   ○ 8 Glass of Water   ○ Balanced Varied Iftar

Iftar & Suhour Meal Planner

Iftar

....
....
....
....

Suhoor

....
....
....
....

To Do List

....
....
....
....

....
....
....
....

How Can I Make Tomorrow Better?

....
....

Daily Reflections

....
....
....
....
....

Rate Your Day   ☆ ☆ ☆ ☆ ☆

Ramadan Day 8

Daily Schedule

Morning

....
....
....

Afternoon

....
....
....

Evening

....
....
....

Night

....
....
....

○ Fajr
○ Asr
○ Isha'a
○ Dhuhr
○ Maghrib
○ Taraweeh

Alhamdulillah for health.
Allah's Messenger ﷺ said: "Allah
pleased with His servant who says: A
Hamdu lillah while taking a morsel
food and while drinking."
(Hadith; Muslim 2734a)

Todays Goals

○ ....
○ ....
○ ....
○ ....
○ ....

Sunnah Habits

○ Morning Dhikr   ○ Exercise   ○ Eat Healthy   ○ Give to Charity
○ Evening Dhikr   ○ 8 Glass of Water   ○ Balanced Varied Iftar

Iftar & Suhour Meal Planner

Iftar

....
....
....
....

Suhoor

....
....
....
....

To Do List

....
....
....
....

....
....
....
....

How Can I Make Tomorrow Better?

....
....

Daily Reflections

....
....
....
....
....
....

Rate Your Day ☆ ☆ ☆ ☆ ☆

Ramadan Day 9

Daily Schedule

Morning

....
....
....
....

Afternoon

....
....
....

Evening

....
....
....
....

Night

....
....
....
....

- ○ Fajr
- ○ Asr
- ○ Isha'a
- ○ Dhuhr
- ○ Maghrib
- ○ Taraweeh

Alhamdulillah for being able to learn good habits.
The Prophet ﷺ used to say "The best amongst you are those who have the best manners and character."
(Hadith; Bukhari 3559)

Todays Goals

- ○ ....
- ○ ....
- ○ ....
- ○ ....
- ○ ....

Sunnah Habits

- ○ Morning Dhikr
- ○ Evening Dhikr
- ○ Exercise
- ○ 8 Glass of Water
- ○ Eat Healthy
- ○ Balanced Varied Iftar
- ○ Give to Charity

Iftar & Suhour Meal Planner

Iftar

....
....
....
....

Suhoor

....
....
....
....

To Do List

....
....
....
....

....
....
....
....

How Can I Make Tomorrow Better?

....
....

Daily Reflections

....
....
....
....
....
....

Rate Your Day ☆ ☆ ☆ ☆ ☆

Ramadan Day 10

Daily Schedule

Morning

....
....
....

Afternoon

....
....
....

Evening

....
....
....

Night

....
....
....

Sunnah Habits

O Morning Dhikr   O Exercise   O Eat Healthy   O Give to Charity
O Evening Dhikr   O 8 Glass of Water O Balanced Varied Iftar

O Fajr
O Asr
O Isha'a
O Dhuhr
O Maghrib
O Taraweeh

Alhamdulillah for being part of the ummah of the Prophet ﷺ.

It was narrated from Asma' bint Yazid that she heard the Messenger of Allah ﷺ say: "Shall I not tell you of the best of you?" They said: "Yes, O Messenger of Allah." He said: "The best of you are those who, when they are seen, Allah the Mighty, the Majestic, is remembered."

(Hadith; Ibn Majah 4119)

Todays Goals

O ....
O ....
O ....
O ....
O ....

Iftar & Suhour Meal Planner

Iftar

....
....
....
....

Suhoor

....
....
....
....

To Do List

....
....
....
....

....
....
....
....

How Can I Make Tomorrow Better?

....
....

Daily Reflections

....
....
....
....
....
....

Rate Your Day ☆ ☆ ☆ ☆ ☆

Ramadan Day 11

Daily Schedule

Morning

....
....
....

Afternoon

....
....
....

Evening

....
....
....

Night

....
....
....

○ Fajr
○ Asr
○ Isha'a
○ Dhuhr
○ Maghrib
○ Taraweeh

Alhamdulillah for being strong.
Allah's Messenger ﷺ said, "The stro
is not the one who overcomes the peopl
by his strength, but the strong is the o
who controls himself while in anger."
(Hadith; Bukhari 6114)

Todays Goals

○ ....
○ ....
○ ....
○ ....
○ ....

Sunnah Habits

○ Morning Dhikr   ○ Exercise   ○ Eat Healthy   ○ Give to Charity
○ Evening Dhikr   ○ 8 Glass of Water   ○ Balanced Varied Iftar

Iftar & Suhour Meal Planner

Iftar

....

....

....

....

Suhoor

....

....

....

....

To Do List

....

....

....

....

....

....

....

....

How Can I Make Tomorrow Better?

....

....

Daily Reflections

....

....

....

....

....

....

Rate Your Day   ☆ ☆ ☆ ☆ ☆

Ramadan Day 12

Daily Schedule

Morning

....
....
....

Afternoon

....
....
....

Evening

....
....
....

Night

....
....
....

- ○ Fajr
- ○ Asr
- ○ Isha'a
- ○ Dhuhr
- ○ Maghrib
- ○ Taraweeh

Alhamdulillah for learning something new daily.
Messenger of Allah ﷺ said: "A place the size of a whip in Paradise is better than this world and everything in it."
(Hadith; Ibn Majah 4330)

Todays Goals

- ○ ....
- ○ ....
- ○ ....
- ○ ....
- ○ ....

Sunnah Habits

- ○ Morning Dhikr
- ○ Evening Dhikr
- ○ Exercise
- ○ 8 Glass of Water
- ○ Eat Healthy
- ○ Balanced Varied Iftar
- ○ Give to Charity

Iftar & Suhour Meal Planner

Iftar

....
....
....
....

Suhoor

....
....
....
....

To Do List

....
....
....
....

....
....
....
....

How Can I Make Tomorrow Better?

....
....

Daily Reflections

....
....
....
....
....
....

Rate Your Day ☆ ☆ ☆ ☆ ☆

Ramadan Day 13

Daily Schedule

Morning
....
....
....

Afternoon
....
....
....

Evening
....
....
....

Night
....
....
....

○ Fajr
○ Asr
○ Isha'a
○ Dhuhr
○ Maghrib
○ Taraweeh

Alhamdulillah for everyday.
Messenger of Allah ﷺ said,
"Whosoever begins the day feeling family security and good health, and possessing provision for his day is as though he possessed the whole world."
(Hadith; Riyad as-Salihin 510)

Todays Goals

○ ....
○ ....
○ ....
○ ....
○ ....

Sunnah Habits

○ Morning Dhikr   ○ Exercise   ○ Eat Healthy   ○ Give to Charity
○ Evening Dhikr   ○ 8 Glass of Water   ○ Balanced Varied Iftar

Iftar & Suhour Meal Planner

Iftar

....

....

....

....

Suhoor

....

....

....

....

To Do List

....

....

....

....

....

....

....

....

How Can I Make Tomorrow Better?

....

....

Daily Reflections

....

....

....

....

....

Rate Your Day ☆ ☆ ☆ ☆ ☆

Ramadan Day 14

Daily Schedule

Morning
....
....
....

Afternoon
....
....
....
....

Evening
....
....
....

Night
....
....
....

O Fajr
O Asr
O Isha'a
O Dhuhr
O Maghrib
O Taraweeh

Alhamdulillah for all the beauty around me. The Prophet ﷺ said, "He who has, in his heart an ant's weight of arrogance will not enter Jannah." Someone said: "A man likes to wear beautiful clothes and shoes?" Messenger of Allah ﷺ said, "Allah is Beautiful, He loves beauty. Arrogance means ridiculing and rejecting the Truth and despising people."
(HADITH; RIYAD AS-SALIHIN 611)

Todays Goals

O ....
O ....
O ....
O ....
O ....

Sunnah Habits

O Morning Dhikr   O Exercise   O Eat Healthy   O Give to Charity
O Evening Dhikr   O 8 Glass of Water   O Balanced Varied Iftar

Iftar & Suhour Meal Planner

Iftar

....

....

....

....

Suhoor

....

....

....

....

To Do List

....

....

....

....

....

....

....

....

How Can I Make Tomorrow Better?

....

....

Daily Reflections

....

....

....

....

....

....

Rate Your Day   ☆ ☆ ☆ ☆ ☆

Ramadan Day 15

Date _____/_____/_____

Daily Schedule

Morning
....
....
....

Afternoon
....
....
....

Evening
....
....
....

Night
....
....
....

- ○ Fajr
- ○ Asr
- ○ Isha'a
- ○ Dhuhr
- ○ Maghrib
- ○ Taraweeh

Alhamdulillah for being able to forgive. The Prophet ﷺ said: "Show mercy and you be shown mercy. Forgive and Allah will forgi you. Woe to the vessels that catchwords (i. the ears). Woe to those who persist and consciously continue in what they are doing. (Hadith; Al-Adab Al-Mufrad 380)

Todays Goals

- ○ ....
- ○ ....
- ○ ....
- ○ ....
- ○ ....

Sunnah Habits

- ○ Morning Dhikr
- ○ Evening Dhikr
- ○ Exercise
- ○ 8 Glass of Water
- ○ Eat Healthy
- ○ Balanced Varied Iftar
- ○ Give to Charity

Iftar & Suhour Meal Planner

Iftar

....

....

....

....

Suhoor

....

....

....

....

To Do List

....

....

....

....

....

....

....

....

How Can I Make Tomorrow Better?

....

....

Daily Reflections

....

....

....

....

....

....

Rate Your Day ☆ ☆ ☆ ☆ ☆

Ramadan Day 16

Daily Schedule

Morning
....
....
....

Afternoon
....
....
....

Evening
....
....
....

Night
....
....
....

O Fajr

O Asr

O Isha'a

O Dhuhr

O Maghrib

O Taraweeh

Alhamdulillah for being able to be thankful.

It was narrated that Thawban said: "When the Verse concerning silver and gold was revealed, they said: 'What kind of wealth should we acquire?' Umar said: 'I will tell you about that.' So he rode on his camel and caught up with the Prophet, and I followed him. He said: 'O Messenger of Allah! what kind of wealth should we acquire?' He said: 'Let one of you acquire a thankful heart, a tongue that remembers Allah and a believing wife who will help him with regard to the Hereafter."

(Hadith; Ibn Majah 12)

Todays Goals

O ....

O ....

O ....

O ....

O ....

Sunnah Habits

O Morning Dhikr   O Exercise   O Eat Healthy   O Give to Charity

O Evening Dhikr   O 8 Glass of Water   O Balanced Varied Iftar

Iftar & Suhour Meal Planner

Iftar

....
....
....
....

Suhoor

....
....
....
....

To Do List

....
....
....
....

....
....
....
....

How Can I Make Tomorrow Better?

....
....

Daily Reflections

....
....
....
....
....
....

Rate Your Day ☆ ☆ ☆ ☆ ☆

Ramadan Day 17

Daily Schedule

Morning

....
....
....

Afternoon

....
....
....

Evening

....
....
....

Night

....
....
....

○ Fajr
○ Asr
○ Isha'a
○ Dhuhr
○ Maghrib
○ Taraweeh

Alhamdulillah for kindness.
'A'isha, the wife of Allah's Apostle ﷺ reported Allah's Apostle ﷺ as saying: "Kindness is not to be found in anything but that it adds to its beauty and it is not withdrawn from anything but it makes it defective."
(Hadith; Muslim 2594a)

Todays Goals

○ ....
○ ....
○ ....
○ ....
○ ....

Sunnah Habits

○ Morning Dhikr   ○ Exercise   ○ Eat Healthy   ○ Give to Charity
○ Evening Dhikr   ○ 8 Glass of Water ○ Balanced Varied Iftar

Iftar & Suhour Meal Planner

Iftar

....
....
....
....

Suhoor

....
....
....
....

To Do List

....
....
....
....

....
....
....
....

How Can I Make Tomorrow Better?

....
....

Daily Reflections

....
....
....
....
....

Rate Your Day ☆ ☆ ☆ ☆ ☆

Ramadan Day 18

Daily Schedule

Morning

....
....
....
....

Afternoon

....
....
....
....

Evening

....
....
....
....

Night

....
....
....
....

○ Fajr
○ Asr
○ Isha'a
○ Dhuhr
○ Maghrib
○ Taraweeh

Alhamdulillah for happiness.
It was narrated from Abu Bakr that when
the Prophet ﷺ heard news that made h
happy, or for which one should be happy,
would fall down in prostration (to show)
gratitude to Allah, the Blessed and Exalte
(Hadith; Ibn Majah 592)

Todays Goals

○ ....
○ ....
○ ....
○ ....
○ ....

Sunnah Habits

○ Morning Dhikr   ○ Exercise   ○ Eat Healthy   ○ Give to Charity
○ Evening Dhikr   ○ 8 Glass of Water   ○ Balanced Varied Iftar

Iftar & Suhour Meal Planner

Iftar

....
....
....
....

Suhoor

....
....
....
....

To Do List

....
....
....
....

....
....
....
....

How Can I Make Tomorrow Better?

....
....

Daily Reflections

....
....
....
....
....
....

Rate Your Day ☆ ☆ ☆ ☆ ☆

Ramadan Day 19

Daily Schedule

Morning
....
....
....

Afternoon
....
....
....

Evening
....
....
....

Night
....
....
....

- O Fajr
- O Asr
- O Isha'a
- O Dhuhr
- O Maghrib
- O Taraweeh

Alhamdulillah for laughter and joy.
Messenger of Allah ﷺ said: "Look at those who are beneath you and do not look at those who are above you, for it is more suitable that you should not consider as less the blessing of Allah."
(Hadith; Ibn Majah 4142)

Todays Goals

- O ....
- O ....
- O ....
- O ....
- O ....

Sunnah Habits

- O Morning Dhikr
- O Evening Dhikr
- O Exercise
- O 8 Glass of Water
- O Eat Healthy
- O Balanced Varied Iftar
- O Give to Charity

Iftar & Suhour Meal Planner

Iftar

....
....
....
....

Suhoor

....
....
....
....

To Do List

....
....
....
....

....
....
....
....

How Can I Make Tomorrow Better?

....
....

Daily Reflections

....
....
....
....
....
....

Rate Your Day ☆ ☆ ☆ ☆ ☆

Ramadan Day 20

Daily Schedule

Morning

....

....

....

Afternoon

....

....

....

Evening

....

....

....

Night

....

....

....

○ Fajr

○ Asr

○ Isha'a

○ Dhuhr

○ Maghrib

○ Taraweeh

Alhamdulillah for having courage

The Messenger of Allah ﷺ said: 'The strong believer is better and more beloved to Allah than the weak believer, although both are good. Strive for that which will benefit you, seek the help of Allah, and do not feel helpless. If anything befalls you, do not say, "if only I had done such and such" rather say "Qaddara Allahu wa ma sha'a fa'ala (Allah has decreed and whatever he wills, He does)." For (saying) 'If' opens (the door) to the deeds of Satan." (Hadith; Ibn Majah 79)

Todays Goals

○ ....

○ ....

○ ....

○ ....

○ ....

Sunnah Habits

○ Morning Dhikr   ○ Exercise   ○ Eat Healthy   ○ Give to Charity

○ Evening Dhikr   ○ 8 Glass of Water   ○ Balanced Varied Iftar

Iftar & Suhour Meal Planner

Iftar
....
....
....
....

Suhoor
....
....
....
....

To Do List
....
....
....
....

....
....
....
....

How Can I Make Tomorrow Better?
....
....

Daily Reflections
....
....
....
....
....
....

Rate Your Day ☆ ☆ ☆ ☆ ☆

Ramadan Day 21

Daily Schedule

Morning
....
....
....

Afternoon
....
....
....

Evening
....
....
....

Night
....
....
....

O Fajr

O Asr

O Isha'a

O Dhuhr

O Maghrib

O Taraweeh

Alhamdulillah for making every day special.

the Messenger of Allah ﷺ said: "Love Allah for what He nourishes you with of H. Blessings, love me due to the love of Allah, and love the people of my house due to love of me."

(Hadith; Tirmidhi 3789)

Todays Goals

O ....
O ....
O ....
O ....
O ....

Sunnah Habits

O Morning Dhikr   O Exercise   O Eat Healthy   O Give to Charity
O Evening Dhikr   O 8 Glass of Water   O Balanced Varied Iftar

Iftar & Suhour Meal Planner

Iftar

....
....
....
....

Suhoor

....
....
....
....

To Do List

....
....
....
....

....
....
....
....

How Can I Make Tomorrow Better?

....
....

Daily Reflections

....
....
....
....
....
....

Rate Your Day ☆ ☆ ☆ ☆ ☆

Ramadan Day 22

Daily Schedule

Morning

....
....
....

Afternoon

....
....
....

Evening

....
....
....

Night

....
....
....

○ Fajr

○ Asr

○ Isha'a

○ Dhuhr

○ Maghrib

○ Taraweeh

Alhamdulillah for being able to mak
an effort.
The Prophet ﷺ said: "He who find
it hard (to recite the Qur'an) will
have a double reward."
(Hadith; Muslim 798b)

Todays Goals

○ ....
○ ....
○ ....
○ ....
○ ....

Sunnah Habits

○ Morning Dhikr   ○ Exercise   ○ Eat Healthy   ○ Give to Charity
○ Evening Dhikr   ○ 8 Glass of Water   ○ Balanced Varied Iftar

Iftar & Suhour Meal Planner

Iftar

....

....

....

....

Suhoor

....

....

....

....

To Do List

....

....

....

....

....

....

....

....

How Can I Make Tomorrow Better?

....

....

Daily Reflections

....

....

....

....

....

Rate Your Day ☆ ☆ ☆ ☆ ☆

Ramadan Day 23

Daily Schedule

Morning
....
....
....

Afternoon
....
....
....

Evening
....
....
....

Night
....
....
....

○ Fajr
○ Asr
○ Isha'a
○ Dhuhr
○ Maghrib
○ Taraweeh

Alhamdulillah for being able to help others.
The Prophet ﷺ said: "None of you believes until he loves for his brother what he loves for himself."
(Hadith; Tirmidhi 2515)

Todays Goals

○ ....
○ ....
○ ....
○ ....
○ ....

Sunnah Habits

○ Morning Dhikr   ○ Exercise   ○ Eat Healthy   ○ Give to Charity
○ Evening Dhikr   ○ 8 Glass of Water   ○ Balanced Varied Iftar

Iftar & Suhour Meal Planner

Iftar

....

....

....

....

Suhoor

....

....

....

....

To Do List

....

....

....

....

....

....

....

....

How Can I Make Tomorrow Better?

....

....

Daily Reflections

....

....

....

....

....

....

Rate Your Day   ☆ ☆ ☆ ☆ ☆

Ramadan Day 24

Daily Schedule

Morning

....
....
....

Afternoon

....
....
....

Evening

....
....
....
....

Night

....
....
....
....

Sunnah Habits

○ Morning Dhikr ○ Exercise ○ Eat Healthy ○ Give to Charity
○ Evening Dhikr ○ 8 Glass of Water ○ Balanced Varied Iftar

○ Fajr
○ Asr
○ Isha'a
○ Dhuhr
○ Maghrib
○ Taraweeh

Alhamdulillah for being able to smile and be rewarded.
Messenger of Allah ﷺ said: "Every good is charity. Indeed among the good is to meet your brother with a smiling face, and to pour what is left in your bucket into the vessel of your brother."
(Hadith; Tirmidhi 1970)

Todays Goals

○ ....
○ ....
○ ....
○ ....
○ ....

Iftar & Suhour Meal Planner

Iftar

....

....

....

....

Suhoor

....

....

....

....

To Do List

....

....

....

....

....

....

....

....

How Can I Make Tomorrow Better?

....

....

Daily Reflections

....

....

....

....

....

Rate Your Day ☆ ☆ ☆ ☆ ☆

Ramadan Day 25

Daily Schedule

Morning

....
....
....
....

Afternoon

....
....
....
....

Evening

....
....
....
....

Night

....
....
....
....

O Fajr

O Asr

O Isha'a

O Dhuhr

O Maghrib

O Taraweeh

Alhamdulillah for being unique.
Narrated Abu Musa: It was said to the
Prophet; "A man may love some people but
he cannot catch up with their good
deeds?" The Prophet ﷺ said, "Everyone
will be with those whom he loves."
(Hadith; Bukhari 6170)

Todays Goals

O ....
O ....
O ....
O ....
O ....

Sunnah Habits

O Morning Dhikr   O Exercise   O Eat Healthy   O Give to Charity
O Evening Dhikr   O 8 Glass of Water   O Balanced Varied Iftar

Iftar & Suhour Meal Planner

Iftar

....

....

....

....

Suhoor

....

....

....

....

To Do List

....

....

....

....

....

....

....

....

How Can I Make Tomorrow Better?

....

....

Daily Reflections

....

....

....

....

....

Rate Your Day ☆ ☆ ☆ ☆ ☆

Date _____/_____/_____

Ramadan Day 26

Daily Schedule

Morning

....
....
....

Afternoon

....
....
....

Evening

....
....
....

Night

....
....
....

○ Fajr
○ Asr
○ Isha'a
○ Dhuhr
○ Maghrib
○ Taraweeh

Alhamdulillah for having people who love me
The Prophet ﷺ said, "If Allah loves a person,
calls Gabriel saying, 'Allah loves so-and-so; O Gab
Love him.' Gabriel would love him and make an
announcement amongst the inhabitants of Heave
'Allah loves so-and-so, therefore you should love
also,' and so all the inhabitants of the Heaven wo
love him, and then he is granted the pleasure of
people on the earth." (Hadith; Bukhari 3209)

Todays Goals

○ ....
○ ....
○ ....
○ ....
○ ....

Sunnah Habits

○ Morning Dhikr   ○ Exercise   ○ Eat Healthy   ○ Give to Charity
○ Evening Dhikr   ○ 8 Glass of Water ○ Balanced Varied Iftar

Iftar & Suhour Meal Planner

Iftar

....
....
....
....

Suhoor

....
....
....
....

To Do List

....
....
....
....

....
....
....
....

How Can I Make Tomorrow Better?

....
....

Daily Reflections

....
....
....
....
....
....

Rate Your Day   ☆ ☆ ☆ ☆ ☆

Ramadan Day 27

Daily Schedule

Morning

....
....
....

Afternoon

....
....
....

Evening

....
....
....

Night

....
....
....

O Fajr

O Asr

O Isha'a

O Dhuhr

O Maghrib

O Taraweeh

Alhamdulillah for praying daily.
the Messenger of Allah ﷺ observe
"The best of the deeds or deed is th
(observance of) prayer at its proper t
and kindness to the parents."
(Hadith, Muslim 85e)

Todays Goals

O ....
O ....
O ....
O ....
O ....

Sunnah Habits

O Morning Dhikr   O Exercise   O Eat Healthy   O Give to Charity
O Evening Dhikr   O 8 Glass of Water O Balanced Varied Iftar

Iftar & Suhour Meal Planner

Iftar

....

....

....

....

Suhoor

....

....

....

....

To Do List

....

....

....

....

....

....

....

....

How Can I Make Tomorrow Better?

....

....

Daily Reflections

....

....

....

....

....

....

Rate Your Day ☆ ☆ ☆ ☆ ☆

Ramadan Day 28

Daily Schedule

Morning

....
....
....

Afternoon

....
....
....

Evening

....
....
....

Night

....
....
....

○ Fajr
○ Asr
○ Isha'a
○ Dhuhr
○ Maghrib
○ Taraweeh

Alhamdulillah for being able to make du
Prophet ﷺ said: "Your Lord is Kind a
Most Generous, and is too kind to let
slave, if he raises his hands to Him, br
them back empty."
(Hadith; Ibn Majah 3865)

Todays Goals

○ ....
○ ....
○ ....
○ ....
○ ....

Sunnah Habits

○ Morning Dhikr   ○ Exercise   ○ Eat Healthy   ○ Give to Charity
○ Evening Dhikr   ○ 8 Glass of Water ○ Balanced Varied Iftar

Iftar & Suhour Meal Planner

Iftar

....
....
....
....

Suhoor

....
....
....
....

To Do List

....
....
....
....

....
....
....
....

How Can I Make Tomorrow Better?

....
....

Daily Reflections

....
....
....
....
....
....

Rate Your Day   ☆ ☆ ☆ ☆ ☆

Ramadan Day 29

Daily Schedule

Morning
....
....
....

Afternoon
....
....
....

Evening
....
....
....
....

Night
....
....
....

○ Fajr
○ Asr
○ Isha'a
○ Dhuhr
○ Maghrib
○ Taraweeh

Alhamdulillah for being loved.
Sahl bin Sa'd As-Sa'idi (May Allah be pleased with him) reported: A man came to the Prophet ﷺ and said, "O Messenger of Allah, guide me to such an action which, if I do Allah will love me and the people will also love me." He ﷺ said, "Have no desire for this world, Allah will love you; and have no desire for what people possess, and the people will love you." (Hadith; Riyad as-Salihin 471)

Todays Goals

○ ....
○ ....
○ ....
○ ....
○ ....

Sunnah Habits

○ Morning Dhikr   ○ Exercise   ○ Eat Healthy   ○ Give to Charity
○ Evening Dhikr   ○ 8 Glass of Water   ○ Balanced Varied Iftar

Iftar & Suhour Meal Planner

Iftar

....
....
....
....

Suhoor

....
....
....
....

To Do List

....
....
....
....

....
....
....
....

How Can I Make Tomorrow Better?

....
....

Daily Reflections

....
....
....
....
....
....

Rate Your Day ☆ ☆ ☆ ☆ ☆

Ramadan Day 30

Date _____ / _____ / _____

Daily Schedule

Morning
....
....
....

Afternoon
....
....
....

Evening
....
....
....

Night
....
....
....

- O Fajr
- O Asr
- O Isha'a
- O Dhuhr
- O Maghrib
- O Taraweeh

Alhamdulillah for having all I need. Allah's Messenger ﷺ said: "Strange are the way a believer for there is good in every affair of his this is not the case with anyone else except in t case of a believer for if he has an occasion to fe delighted, he thanks (God), thus there is a good him in it, and if he gets into trouble and shows resignation (and endures it patiently), there is a for him in it." (Hadith; Muslim 2999)

Todays Goals

- O ....
- O ....
- O ....
- O ....
- O ....

Sunnah Habits

- O Morning Dhikr
- O Evening Dhikr
- O Exercise
- O 8 Glass of Water
- O Eat Healthy
- O Balanced Varied Iftar
- O Give to Charity

Iftar & Suhour Meal Planner

Iftar

....
....
....
....

Suhoor

....
....
....
....

To Do List

....
....
....
....

....
....
....
....

How Can I Make Tomorrow Better?

....
....

Daily Reflections

....
....
....
....
....
....

Rate Your Day   ☆ ☆ ☆ ☆ ☆

A Dua a Day and Notes

1- LOVE

اللَّهُمَّ حَبِّبْ إِلَيْنَا الإِيمَانَ وَزَيَّنْهُ فِي قُلُوبِنَا ... اللَّهُمَّ تَوَفَّنَا مُسْلِمِينَ، وَأَحْيِنَا مُسْلِمِينَ، وَأَلْحِقْنَا بِالصَّالِحِينَ، غَيْرَ خَزَايَا وَلاَ مَفْتُونِينَ

O Allah, make us love belief and adorn our hearts with it...O Allah, make..." us die Muslims and make us live as Muslims and join us to the rightly, acting, (who are neither disappointed nor afflicted." (Hadith; Al-Adab Al-Mufrad

A Dua a Day and Notes

2- HUMBLENESS

اللَّهُمَّ إِنِّي أَعُوذُ بِكَ مِنْ عِلْمٍ لاَ يَنْفَعُ وَمِنْ قَلْبٍ لاَ يَخْشَعُ وَمِنْ نَفْسٍ لاَ تَشْبَعُ وَمِنْ دُعَاءٍ لاَ يُسْمَعُ

"O Allah, I seek refuge with You from the knowledge that is of no benefit, a heart that is not humble, a soul that is not satisfied, and a supplication that is not heard." (Hadith; Nasa'i 5536)

....

....

....

....

....

....

....

....

....

....

....

....

....

....

A Dua a Day and Notes

3- SELF-SUFFICIENCY

اللَّهُمَّ إِنِّي أَسْأَلُكَ الْهُدَى وَالتُّقَى وَالْعَفَافَ وَالْغِنَى

"O Allah, indeed, I ask You for guidance, piety, chastity, and self-sufficiency." (Hadith; Tirmidhi 3489)

....
....
....
....
....
....
....
....
....
....
....
....
....
....
....
....
....
....

A Dua a Day and Notes

4- WISDOM

اَللَّهُمَّ اِنْفَعْنِي بِمَا عَلَّمْتَنِي، وَعَلِّمْنِي مَا يَنْفَعُنِي، وَارْزُقْنِي عِلْمًا يَنْفَعُنِي

"O Allah! Grant me benefit in what you have taught me, and teach me useful knowledge and provide me with the knowledge that will benefit me." (Bulugh al-Maram)

A Dua a Day and Notes

5- PROTECTION

أَعُوذُ بِكَلِمَاتِ اللَّهِ التَّامَّاتِ مِنْ شَرِّ مَا خَلَقَ

"I seek refuge in Allah's Perfect Words from the evil of what he created." (Hadith; Tirmidhi 3604b)

··

··

··

··

··

··

··

··

··

··

··

··

··

··

··

··

··

A Dua a Day and Notes

6- FORGIVENESS

رَبِّ اجْعَلْنِي مُقِيمَ الصَّلَاةِ وَمِن ذُرِّيَّتِي رَبَّنَا وَتَقَبَّلْ دُعَاءِ
رَبَّنَا اغْفِرْ لِي وَلِوَالِدَيَّ وَلِلْمُؤْمِنِينَ يَوْمَ يَقُومُ الْحِسَابُ

"My Lord, make me an establisher of prayer, and from my descendants. Our Lord, and accept my supplication. Our Lord, forgive me and my parents and the believers the Day the account is established." (Quran; 14:40-41)

....
....
....
....
....
....
....
....
....
....
....
....
....
....
....
....
....
....

7- KINDNESS

اَللَّهُمَّ كَمَا أَحْسَنْتَ خَلْقِي، فَحَسِّنْ خُلُقِي

"O Allah You have made my creation perfect, so make my moral characteristics also the best." (Hadith; Bulugh al-Maram)

A Dua a Day and Notes

8- GUIDANCE

اللَّهُمَّ اجْعَلْ فِي قَلْبِي نُورًا وَفِي سَمْعِي نُورًا وَفِي بَصَرِي نُورًا وَعَنْ يَمِينِي نُورًا وَعَنْ شِمَالِي نُورًا وَأَمَامِي نُورًا وَخَلْفِي نُورًا وَفَوْقِي نُورًا وَتَحْتِي نُورًا وَاجْعَلْ لِي نُورًا

"O Allah! place light in my heart, light in my hearing, light in my sight, light on my right, light on my left, light in front of me, light behind me, light above me, light below me, make light for me." [Hadith; Muslim 763 g]

9- GRATITUDE

رَبِّ أَوْزِعْنِي أَنْ أَشْكُرَ نِعْمَتَكَ الَّتِي أَنْعَمْتَ عَلَيَّ وَعَلَى وَالِدَيَّ وَأَنْ أَعْمَلَ صَالِحًا تَرْضَاهُ وَأَصْلِحْ لِي فِي ذُرِّيَّتِي إِنِّي تُبْتُ إِلَيْكَ وَإِنِّي مِنَ الْمُسْلِمِينَ

"My Lord, enable me to be grateful for Your favor which You have bestowed upon me and upon my parents and to work righteousness of which You will approve and make righteous for me my offspring. Indeed, I have repented to You, and indeed, I am of the Muslims."
(Quran; 46:15)

....
....
....
....
....
....
....
....
....
....
....
....

A Dua a Day and Notes

10- SUCCESS

رَبَّنَا آتِنَا فِي الدُّنْيَا حَسَنَةً وَفِي الْآخِرَةِ حَسَنَةً وَقِنَا عَذَابَ النَّارِ

"Our Lord, give us in this world good and in the Hereafter good and protect us from the punishment of the Fire." (Quran; 2:201)

....

....

....

....

....

....

....

....

....

....

....

....

....

....

....

....

A Dua a Day and Notes

11- REPENTANCE

اللَّهُمَّ اغْفِرْ لِي ذَنْبِي كُلَّهُ دِقَّهُ وَجِلَّهُ وَأَوَّلَهُ وَآخِرَهُ وَعَلاَنِيَتَهُ وَسِرَّهُ

"O Lord, forgive me all my sins, small and great, first and last, open and secret." (Hadith; Muslim 483)

....
....
....
....
....
....
....
....
....
....
....
....
....
....
....
....
....

A Dua a Day and Notes

12- MINDFULNESS

رَبِّ أَعِنِّي عَلَى ذِكْرِكَ وَشُكْرِكَ وَحُسْنِ عِبَادَتِكَ

"My Lord, help me to remember You, give thanks to You and worship You well." (Hadith; Nasa'i 1303)

....
....
....
....
....
....
....
....
....
....
....
....
....
....
....
....
....

A Dua a Day and Notes

13- SECURITY

اَللَّهُمَّ إِنِّي أَسْأَلُكَ اَلْعَافِيَةَ فِي دِينِي، وَدُنْيَايَ، وَأَهْلِي، وَمَالِي، اَللَّهُمَّ اسْتُرْ عَوْرَاتِي، وَآمِنْ رَوْعَاتِي، وَاحْفَظْنِي مِنْ بَيْنِ يَدَيَّ، وَمِنْ خَلْفِي، وَعَنْ يَمِينِي، وَعَنْ شِمَالِي، وَمِنْ فَوْقِي، وَأَعُوذُ بِعَظَمَتِكَ أَنْ أُغْتَالَ مِنْ تَحْتِي

"O Allah! I ask you for pardon and well-being in my religious and worldly affairs, and my family and my wealth. O Allah! Cover my weaknesses and set at ease my dismay. O Allah! Preserve me from the front and from behind and on my right and on my left and from above, and I seek refuge with you lest I be swallowed up by the earth." (Hadith; Bulugh al-Maram)

A Dua a Day and Notes

14- ACCEPTANCE

رَبَّنَا تَقَبَّلْ مِنَّا إِنَّكَ أَنتَ السَّمِيعُ الْعَلِيمُ

"Our Lord, accept from us. Indeed You are the Hearing, the Knowing." (Quran; 2:127)

15- RIGHTEOUSNESS

رَبَّنَا هَبْ لَنَا مِنْ أَزْوَاجِنَا وَذُرِّيَّاتِنَا قُرَّةَ أَعْيُنٍ وَاجْعَلْنَا لِلْمُتَّقِينَ إِمَامًا

"Our Lord, grant us from among our wives and offspring comfort to our eyes and make us an example for the righteous." (Quran; 25:74)

_____

_____

_____

_____

_____

_____

_____

_____

_____

_____

_____

_____

_____

_____

_____

_____

A Dua a Day and Notes

16- PEACE

اللَّهُمَّ إِنِّي أَعُوذُ بِكَ مِنَ الْبُخْلِ وَالْجُبْنِ وَأَعُوذُ بِكَ مِنْ سُوءِ الْعُمُرِ وَأَعُوذُ بِكَ مِنْ فِتْنَةِ الصَّدْرِ وَأَعُوذُ بِكَ مِنْ عَذَابِ الْقَبْرِ

"O Allah, I seek refuge with You from miserliness and cowardice, and I seek refuge with You from reaching the age of second childhood, and I seek refuge in You from the ills of the heart, and I seek refuge in You from the torment of the grave." (Hadith; Nasa'i 5497)

17- COMPASSION

اللَّهُمَّ إِنِّي أَسْأَلُكَ فِعْلَ الْخَيْرَاتِ وَتَرْكَ الْمُنْكَرَاتِ وَحُبَّ الْمَسَاكِينِ وَأَنْ تَغْفِرَ لِي وَتَرْحَمَنِي وَإِذَا أَرَدْتَ فِتْنَةَ قَوْمٍ فَتَوَفَّنِي غَيْرَ مَفْتُونٍ أَسْأَلُكَ حُبَّكَ وَحُبَّ مَنْ يُحِبُّكَ وَحُبَّ عَمَلٍ يُقَرِّبُ إِلَى حُبِّكَ

"O Allah! I ask of you the doing of the good deeds, avoiding the evil deeds, loving the poor, and that You forgive me, and have mercy upon me. And when You have willed Fitnah in the people, then take me without the Fitnah. And I ask You for Your love, the love of whomever You love, and the love of the deeds that bring one nearer to Your love." (Hadith; Tirmidhi)

....
....
....
....
....
....
....
....
....
....
....
....

A Dua a Day and Notes

18- BARAKAH

اللَّهُمَّ اجْعَلْ مَعَ الْبَرَكَةِ بَرَكَتَيْنِ

"O Allah, shower with its blessings two other blessings (multiply blessings showered upon it)." [Hadith; Muslim 1374 b]

....

....

....

....

....

....

....

....

....

....

....

....

....

....

....

....

....

A Dua a Day and Notes

19- TRUTHFULNESS

اللَّهُمَّ إِنِّي أَسْأَلُكَ الثَّبَاتَ فِي الأُمْرِ وَالْعَزِيمَةِ عَلَى الرُّشْدِ وَأَسْأَلُكَ شُكْرَ نِعْمَتِكَ وَحُسْنَ عِبَادَتِكَ وَأَسْأَلُكَ قَلْبًا سَلِيمًا وَلِسَانًا صَادِقًا وَأَسْأَلُكَ مِنْ خَيْرِ مَا تَعْلَمُ وَأَعُوذُ بِكَ مِنْ شَرِّ مَا تَعْلَمُ وَأَسْتَغْفِرُكَ لِمَا تَعْلَمُ

"O Allah, I ask You for steadfastness in all my affairs and determination in following the right path, I ask You to make me thankful for Your blessings and to make me worship You properly. I ask You for a sound heart and a truthful tongue. I ask You for the best of what You know and I seek refuge in You from the worst of what You know and I seek Your forgiveness for what You know." (Hadith; Nasa'i 1304)

....
....
....
....
....
....
....
....
....
....

A Dua a Day and Notes

20- POSITIVITY

اللَّهُمَّ اجْعَلْنِي أَعَظِّمُ شُكْرَكَ وَأُكْثِرُ ذِكْرَكَ وَأَتَّبِعُ نَصِيحَتَكَ وَأَحْفَظُ وَصِيَّتَكَ

"O Allah, make me revere gratitude to You, make me increase in remembrance to You, make me follow Your advice, and (make me) guard over that which you have commanded."
(Hadith; Tirmidhi 3604c)

....
....
....
....
....
....
....
....
....
....
....
....
....
....
....
....
....
....
....

21- BENEVOLENCE

اللَّهُمَّ اهْدِنِي لِأَحْسَنِ الْأَعْمَالِ وَأَحْسَنِ الْأَخْلَاقِ لاَ يَهْدِي لِأَحْسَنِهَا إِلاَّ أَنْتَ وَقِنِي سَيِّئَ الْأَعْمَالِ وَسَيِّئَ الْأَخْلَاقِ لاَ يَقِي سَيِّئَهَا إِلاَّ أَنْتَ

"O Allah, guide me to the best of deeds and the best of manners, for none can guide to the best of them but You. And protect me from bad deeds and bad manners, for none can protect against them but You." (Hadith; Nasa'i 896)

A Dua a Day and Notes

22- TAWAKKAL

اللَّهُمَّ اهْدِنِي فِيمَنْ هَدَيْتَ وَعَافِنِي فِيمَنْ عَافَيْتَ وَتَوَلَّنِي فِيمَنْ تَوَلَّيْتَ وَبَارِكْ لِي فِيمَا أَعْطَيْتَ وَقِنِي شَرَّ مَا قَضَيْتَ فَإِنَّكَ تَقْضِي وَلَا يُقْضَى عَلَيْكَ وَإِنَّهُ لَا يَذِلُّ مَنْ وَالَيْتَ تَبَارَكْتَ رَبَّنَا وَتَعَالَيْتَ

"O Allah guide me among those You have guided, pardon me among those You have pardoned, befriend me among those You have befriended, bless me in what You have granted, and save me from the evil that You decreed. Indeed You decree, and none can pass decree, and none can pass decree upon You, indeed he is not humiliated whom You have befriended, blessed are You our Lord and Exalted." (Hadith; Tirmidhi 464)

23- EASE

اللَّهُمَّ اغْفِرْ لِحَيِّنَا وَمَيِّتِنَا وَصَغِيرِنَا وَكَبِيرِنَا وَذَكَرِنَا وَأُنْثَانَا وَشَاهِدِنَا وَغَائِبِنَا اللَّهُمَّ مَنْ أَحْيَيْتَهُ مِنَّا فَأَحْيِهِ عَلَى الإِيمَانِ وَمَنْ تَوَفَّيْتَهُ مِنَّا فَتَوَفَّهُ عَلَى الإِسْلاَمِ اللَّهُمَّ لاَ تَحْرِمْنَا أَجْرَهُ وَلاَ تُضِلَّنَا بَعْدَهُ

"O Allah, forgive those of us who are living and those of us who are dead, those of us who are present and those of us who are absent, our young and our old, our male and our female. O Allah, to whomsoever of us Thou givest life grant him life as a believer, and whomsoever of us Thou takest in death take him in death as a follower of Islam. O Allah, do not withhold from us the reward (of faith) and do not lead us astray after his death."
(Hadith; Abi Dawud 3201)

....
....
....
....
....
....
....
....
....
....
....

A Dua a Day and Notes

24- DIRECTION

اللَّهُمَّ اهْدِنِي وَسَدِّدْنِي

"O Allah, direct me to the right path and make me adhere to the straight path." (Hadith; Muslim 2725 a)

....

....

....

....

....

....

....

....

....

....

....

....

....

....

....

....

....

....

A Dua a Day and Notes

25- CONTENTMENT

رَبِّ إِنِّي لِمَا أَنزَلْتَ إِلَيَّ مِنْ خَيْرٍ فَقِيرٌ

"My Lord, indeed I am, for whatever good You would send down to me, in need." (Quran; 28:24)

....
....
....
....
....
....
....
....
....
....
....
....
....
....
....
....
....
....

A Dua a Day and Notes

26- JANNAH

رَبِّ ابْنِ لِي عِندَكَ بَيْتًا فِي الْجَنَّة

"My Lord, build for me near You a house in Paradise..." (Quran; 66:11)

A Dua a Day and Notes

27- SELF-CONTROL

اللَّهُمَّ رَحْمَتَكَ أَرْجُو فَلاَ تَكِلْنِي إِلَى نَفْسِي طَرْفَةَ عَيْنٍ وَأَصْلِحْ لِي شَأْنِي كُلَّهُ لاَ إِلَهَ إِلاَّ أَنْتَ

"O Allah! Your mercy is what I hope for. Do not abandon me to myself for an instant, but put all my affairs in good order for me. There is no god but You." (Hadith; Abi Dawud 5090)

A Dua a Day and Notes

28- PATIENCE

رَبَّنَا أَفْرِغْ عَلَيْنَا صَبْرًا وَتَوَفَّنَا مُسْلِمِينَ

"Our Lord, pour upon us patience and let us die as Muslims ." [Quran; 7:126]

....
....
....
....
....
....
....
....
....
....
....
....
....
....
....
....
....
....

A Dua a Day and Notes

29- VIRTUE

اللَّهُمَّ أَصْلِحْ لِي دِينِيَ الَّذِي هُوَ عِصْمَةُ أَمْرِي وَأَصْلِحْ لِي دُنْيَايَ الَّتِي فِيهَا مَعَاشِي وَأَصْلِحْ لِي آخِرَتِي الَّتِي فِيهَا مَعَادِي وَاجْعَلِ الْحَيَاةَ زِيَادَةً لِي فِي كُلِّ خَيْرٍ وَاجْعَلِ الْمَوْتَ رَاحَةً لِي مِنْ كُلِّ شَرٍّ

"O Allah, set right for me my religion which is the safeguard of my affairs. And set right for me the affairs of my world wherein is my living. And set right for me my Hereafter on which depends my after-life. And make the life for me (a source) of abundance for every good and make my death a source of comfort for me protecting me against every evil."
(Hadith; Muslim 2720)

....

....

....

....

....

....

....

....

....

....

....

....

A Dua a Day and Notes

30- PURITY

اللَّهُمَّ آتِ نَفْسِي تَقْوَاهَا وَزَكِّهَا أَنْتَ خَيْرُ مَنْ زَكَّاهَا أَنْتَ وَلِيُّهَا وَمَوْلَاهَا

"O Allah, make my soul obedient and purify it, for You are the best One to purify it, You are its Guardian and Lord." (Hadith; Nasa'i 5458)

....

....

....

....

....

....

....

....

....

....

....

....

....

....

....

....

Iftar Party Planner

Date : _____

Invite Time : _____

Maghrib Time : _____

Invite List

- ○ _____
- ○ _____
- ○ _____
- ○ _____
- ○ _____
- ○ _____
- ○ _____
- ○ _____
- ○ _____
- ○ _____

Groceries

- ○ _____
- ○ _____
- ○ _____
- ○ _____
- ○ _____
- ○ _____
- ○ _____
- ○ _____
- ○ _____
- ○ _____
- ○ _____
- ○ _____
- ○ _____
- ○ _____
- ○ _____
- ○ _____
- ○ _____
- ○ _____
- ○ _____
- ○ _____
- ○ _____
- ○ _____

Menu

- ○ _____   ○ _____
- ○ _____   ○ _____
- ○ _____   ○ _____
- ○ _____   ○ _____
- ○ _____   ○ _____
- ○ _____   ○ _____
- ○ _____   ○ _____
- ○ _____   ○ _____
- ○ _____   ○ _____
- ○ _____   ○ _____

Iftar Party Planner

Date : _____

Invite Time : _____

Maghrib Time : _____

Invite List

- ○ _____
- ○ _____
- ○ _____
- ○ _____
- ○ _____
- ○ _____
- ○ _____
- ○ _____
- ○ _____
- ○ _____

Menu

- ○ _____   ○ _____
- ○ _____   ○ _____
- ○ _____   ○ _____
- ○ _____   ○ _____
- ○ _____   ○ _____
- ○ _____   ○ _____
- ○ _____   ○ _____
- ○ _____   ○ _____
- ○ _____   ○ _____

Groceries

- ○ _____
- ○ _____
- ○ _____
- ○ _____
- ○ _____
- ○ _____
- ○ _____
- ○ _____
- ○ _____
- ○ _____
- ○ _____
- ○ _____
- ○ _____
- ○ _____
- ○ _____
- ○ _____
- ○ _____
- ○ _____
- ○ _____
- ○ _____
- ○ _____
- ○ _____
- ○ _____
- ○ _____
- ○ _____
- ○ _____

Iftar Party Planner

Date : _____

Invite Time : _____

Maghrib Time : _____

Invite List

- ○ _____
- ○ _____
- ○ _____
- ○ _____
- ○ _____
- ○ _____
- ○ _____
- ○ _____
- ○ _____
- ○ _____

Groceries

- ○ _____
- ○ _____
- ○ _____
- ○ _____
- ○ _____
- ○ _____
- ○ _____
- ○ _____
- ○ _____
- ○ _____
- ○ _____
- ○ _____
- ○ _____
- ○ _____
- ○ _____
- ○ _____
- ○ _____
- ○ _____
- ○ _____
- ○ _____
- ○ _____
- ○ _____

Menu

- ○ _____   ○ _____
- ○ _____   ○ _____
- ○ _____   ○ _____
- ○ _____   ○ _____
- ○ _____   ○ _____
- ○ _____   ○ _____
- ○ _____   ○ _____
- ○ _____   ○ _____
- ○ _____   ○ _____
- ○ _____   ○ _____

Iftar Party Planner

Date : _____

Invite Time : _____

Maghrib Time : _____

Invite List

- ○ _____
- ○ _____
- ○ _____
- ○ _____
- ○ _____
- ○ _____
- ○ _____
- ○ _____
- ○ _____
- ○ _____
- ○ _____

Groceries

- ○ _____
- ○ _____
- ○ _____
- ○ _____
- ○ _____
- ○ _____
- ○ _____
- ○ _____
- ○ _____
- ○ _____
- ○ _____
- ○ _____
- ○ _____
- ○ _____
- ○ _____
- ○ _____
- ○ _____
- ○ _____
- ○ _____
- ○ _____
- ○ _____
- ○ _____
- ○ _____
- ○ _____
- ○ _____

Menu

- ○ _____   ○ _____
- ○ _____   ○ _____
- ○ _____   ○ _____
- ○ _____   ○ _____
- ○ _____   ○ _____
- ○ _____   ○ _____
- ○ _____   ○ _____
- ○ _____   ○ _____
- ○ _____   ○ _____
- ○ _____   ○ _____

Iftar Party Planner

Date : _____

Invite Time : _____

Maghrib Time : _____

Invite List

- ○ _____
- ○ _____
- ○ _____
- ○ _____
- ○ _____
- ○ _____
- ○ _____
- ○ _____
- ○ _____
- ○ _____

Groceries

- ○ _____
- ○ _____
- ○ _____
- ○ _____
- ○ _____
- ○ _____
- ○ _____
- ○ _____
- ○ _____
- ○ _____
- ○ _____
- ○ _____
- ○ _____
- ○ _____
- ○ _____
- ○ _____
- ○ _____
- ○ _____
- ○ _____
- ○ _____
- ○ _____
- ○ _____

Menu

- ○ _____
- ○ _____
- ○ _____
- ○ _____
- ○ _____
- ○ _____
- ○ _____
- ○ _____
- ○ _____
- ○ _____

- ○ _____
- ○ _____
- ○ _____
- ○ _____
- ○ _____
- ○ _____
- ○ _____
- ○ _____
- ○ _____
- ○ _____

Iftar Party Planner

Date : _____

Invite Time : _____

Maghrib Time : _____

Invite List

- ○ _____
- ○ _____
- ○ _____
- ○ _____
- ○ _____
- ○ _____
- ○ _____
- ○ _____
- ○ _____
- ○ _____
- ○ _____
- ○ _____

Groceries

- ○ _____
- ○ _____
- ○ _____
- ○ _____
- ○ _____
- ○ _____
- ○ _____
- ○ _____
- ○ _____
- ○ _____
- ○ _____
- ○ _____
- ○ _____
- ○ _____
- ○ _____
- ○ _____
- ○ _____
- ○ _____
- ○ _____
- ○ _____
- ○ _____
- ○ _____
- ○ _____

Menu

○ _____	○ _____
○ _____	○ _____
○ _____	○ _____
○ _____	○ _____
○ _____	○ _____
○ _____	○ _____
○ _____	○ _____
○ _____	○ _____
○ _____	○ _____
○ _____	○ _____

Iftar Party Planner

Date : _____

Invite Time : _____

Maghrib Time : _____

Invite List

- _____
- _____
- _____
- _____
- _____
- _____
- _____
- _____
- _____
- _____

Menu

- _____ - _____
- _____ - _____
- _____ - _____
- _____ - _____
- _____ - _____
- _____ - _____
- _____ - _____
- _____ - _____
- _____ - _____
- _____ - _____

Groceries

- _____
- _____
- _____
- _____
- _____
- _____
- _____
- _____
- _____
- _____
- _____
- _____
- _____
- _____
- _____
- _____
- _____
- _____
- _____
- _____
- _____
- _____
- _____
- _____

Iftar Party Planner

Date : _____

Invite Time : _____

Maghrib Time : _____

Invite List

- _____
- _____
- _____
- _____
- _____
- _____
- _____
- _____
- _____
- _____

Groceries

- _____
- _____
- _____
- _____
- _____
- _____
- _____
- _____
- _____
- _____
- _____
- _____
- _____
- _____
- _____
- _____
- _____
- _____
- _____
- _____
- _____
- _____
- _____
- _____
- _____
- _____

Menu

- _____ - _____
- _____ - _____
- _____ - _____
- _____ - _____
- _____ - _____
- _____ - _____
- _____ - _____
- _____ - _____
- _____ - _____
- _____ - _____

Aid Preparation

Gifts To Buy

The Days Plan

What To Wear

Food To Make

Aid Preparation

Gifts To Buy

The Days Plan

What To Wear

Food To Make

Thank You For
Buying This Book
DON'T FORGET TO RATE
THIS PLANNER AND GIVE
US YOUR OPINION

رمضان كريم

Karim Hussain

Made in the USA
Las Vegas, NV
09 March 2024

86838986R00061